DK READERS

READING 3 ALONE

THE **X-MEN** SCHOOL

Written by Michael Teitelbaum

DK

DK Publishing, Inc.

Who are the X-Men?

The X-Men are mutants. What is a mutant? A mutant is someone with special powers. Some mutants can fly, others can create ice, shoot energy beams from their eyes, or control the weather. Some have great mental powers and can read minds.

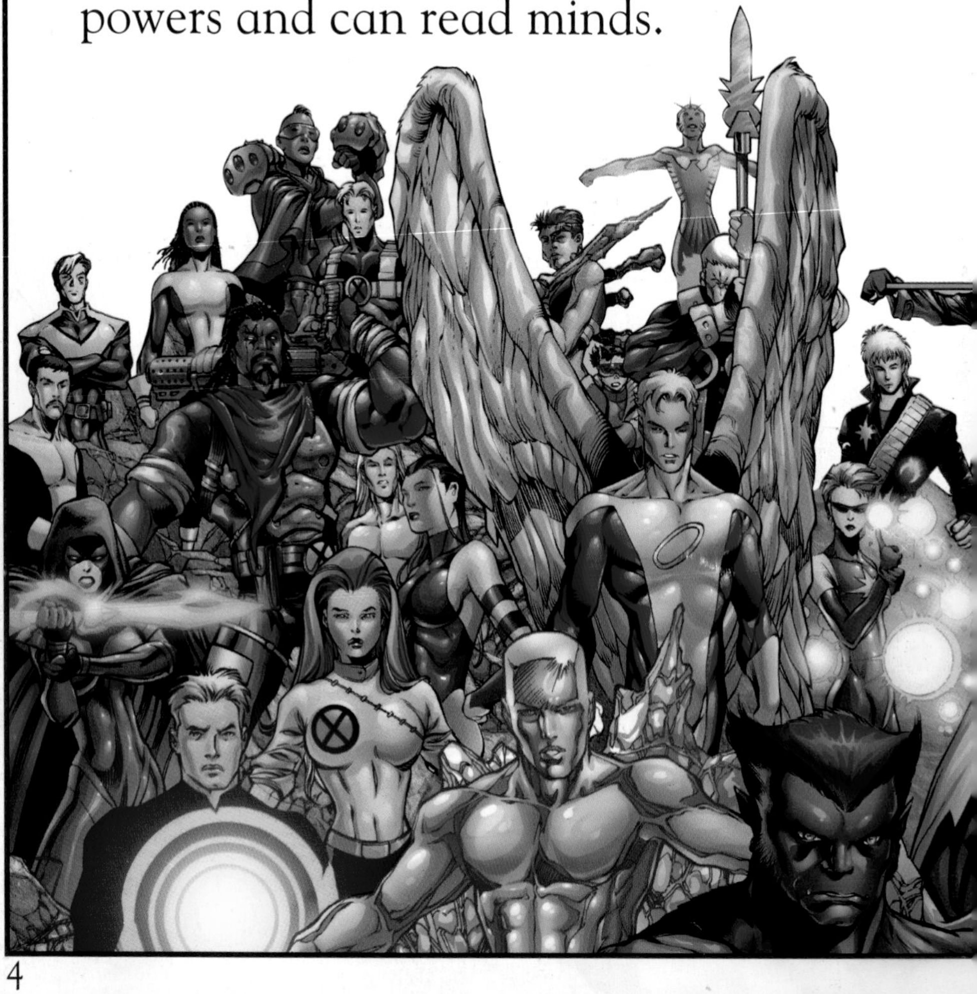

Mutants are people who have evolved to a higher level than ordinary humans. Their special powers usually emerge when they are children. Many have trouble controlling their powers.
Some are scared by their amazing abilities.

One man decided to help the mutants and bring them together as the X-Men.

Over the years, many mutants have joined the X-Men.

Professor X

Professor Charles Xavier is the man who brought the X-Men together. His students know him as Professor X. He is also a mutant and has great mental powers.

Name game
The X-Men got their
name from their leader,
Professor X. The "X" also
stands for the extra power
that mutants have.

He can read the minds of other people. He can also send messages into people's minds. Professor X can make people believe they are seeing or hearing things that aren't really there. His mental powers can be used to stop people from moving or to take away their memories.

Professor X can no longer walk because an alien called Lucifer dropped a massive stone block on him in a fight.

The school

Most mutants just want to get along with humans and be accepted for who they are. But many humans treat them badly. They are afraid of mutants, believing that they are a threat to humans.

Humans are also afraid of mutants because they are different. Some humans want mutants to live apart from them.

Professor X believes that humans and mutants should live together in peace. He hopes that humans can learn not to fear mutants but to treat them as friends with special gifts.

Because of this belief, Professor X started his School for Gifted Youngsters.

The X-Men member Angel rescues a mutant girl from an angry crowd.

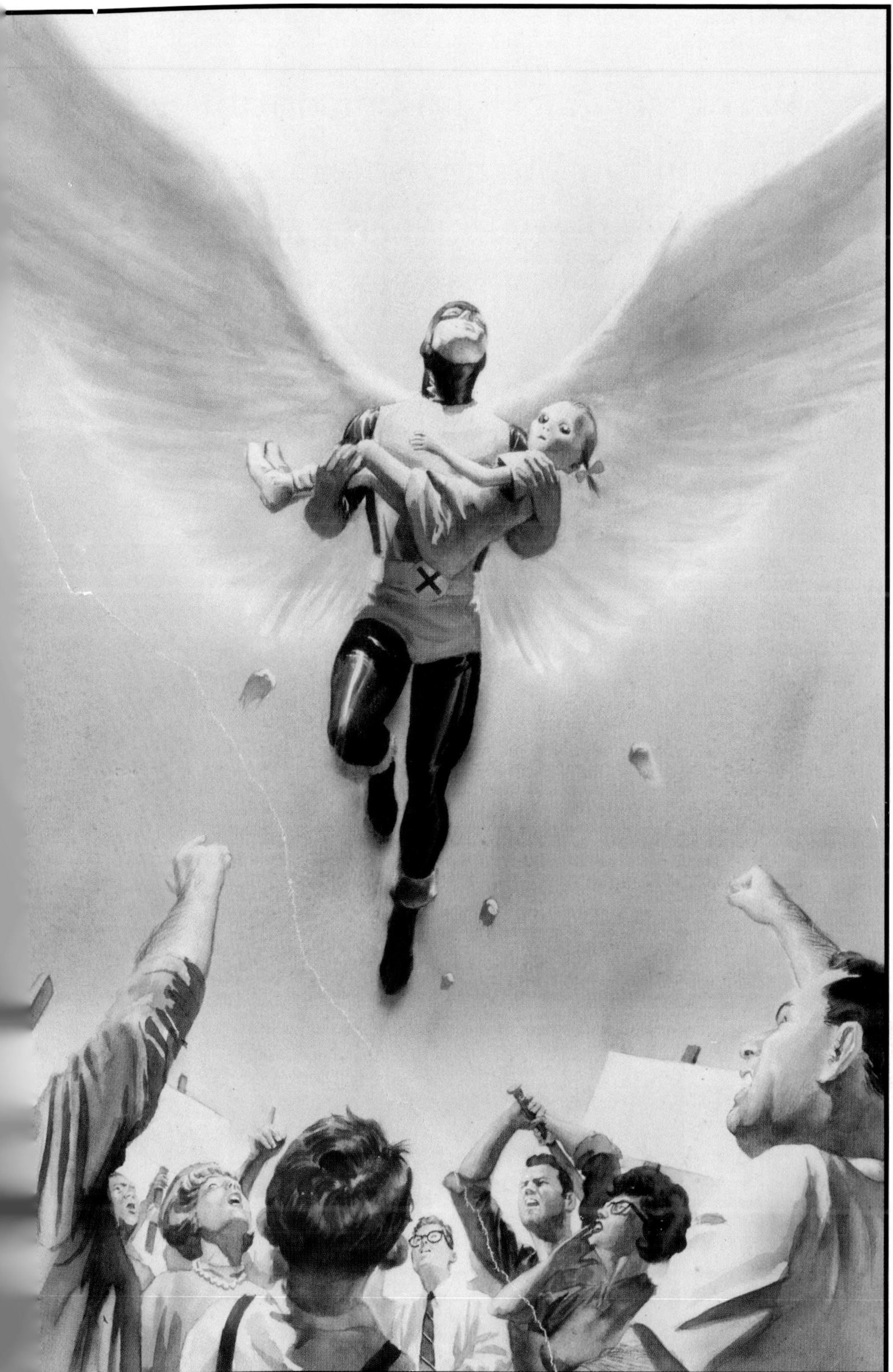

Professor X feels it is important for young mutants to have a place where they can learn to use their powers alongside others like themselves. At his School for Gifted Youngsters, they can study in safety, away from human prejudice and hatred.

There, frightened young mutants who are just discovering their powers find comfort and friendship among others like them.

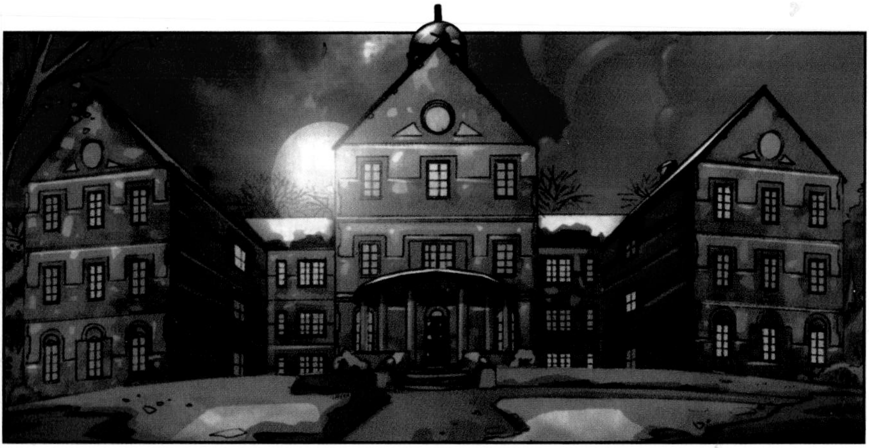

They also find a great teacher in Professor X. The professor trains his students to control their powers and to use them only for good.

The students at the school have many different powers.

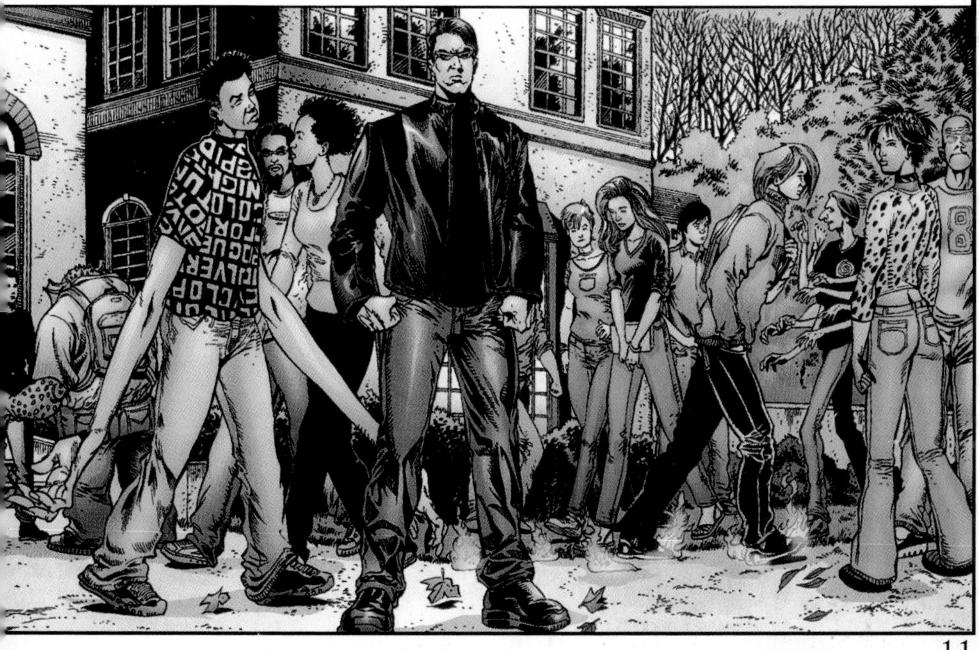

The mansion

Professor X owns a large private estate in Westchester County, north of New York City, that includes a great mansion. The professor uses this house and land as the home for his school.

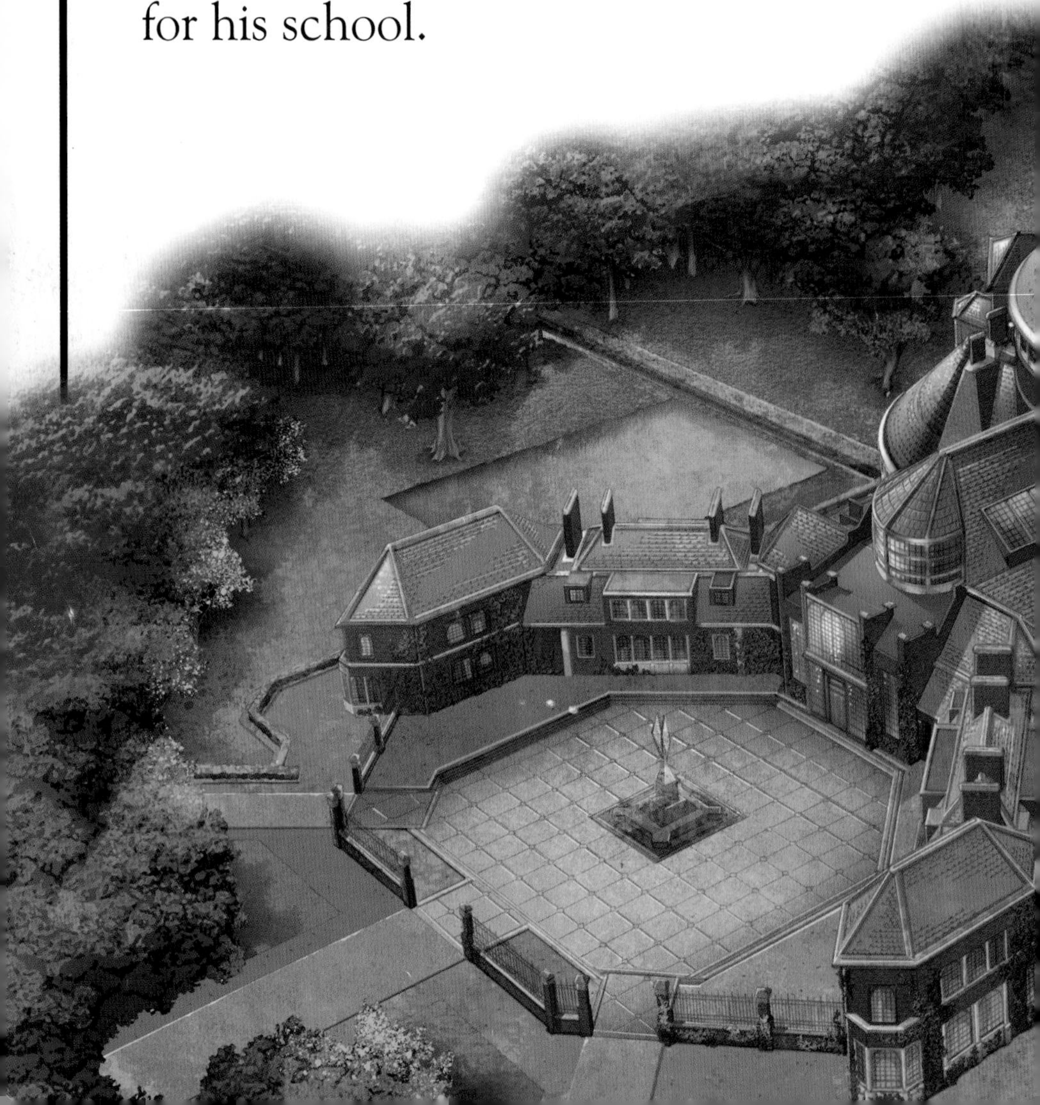

Security is very important at the school. Professor X installed a steel front gate protected by an invisible force field. The beautiful grounds of the estate contain a swimming pool, stables, lakes, a boathouse, and a maze.

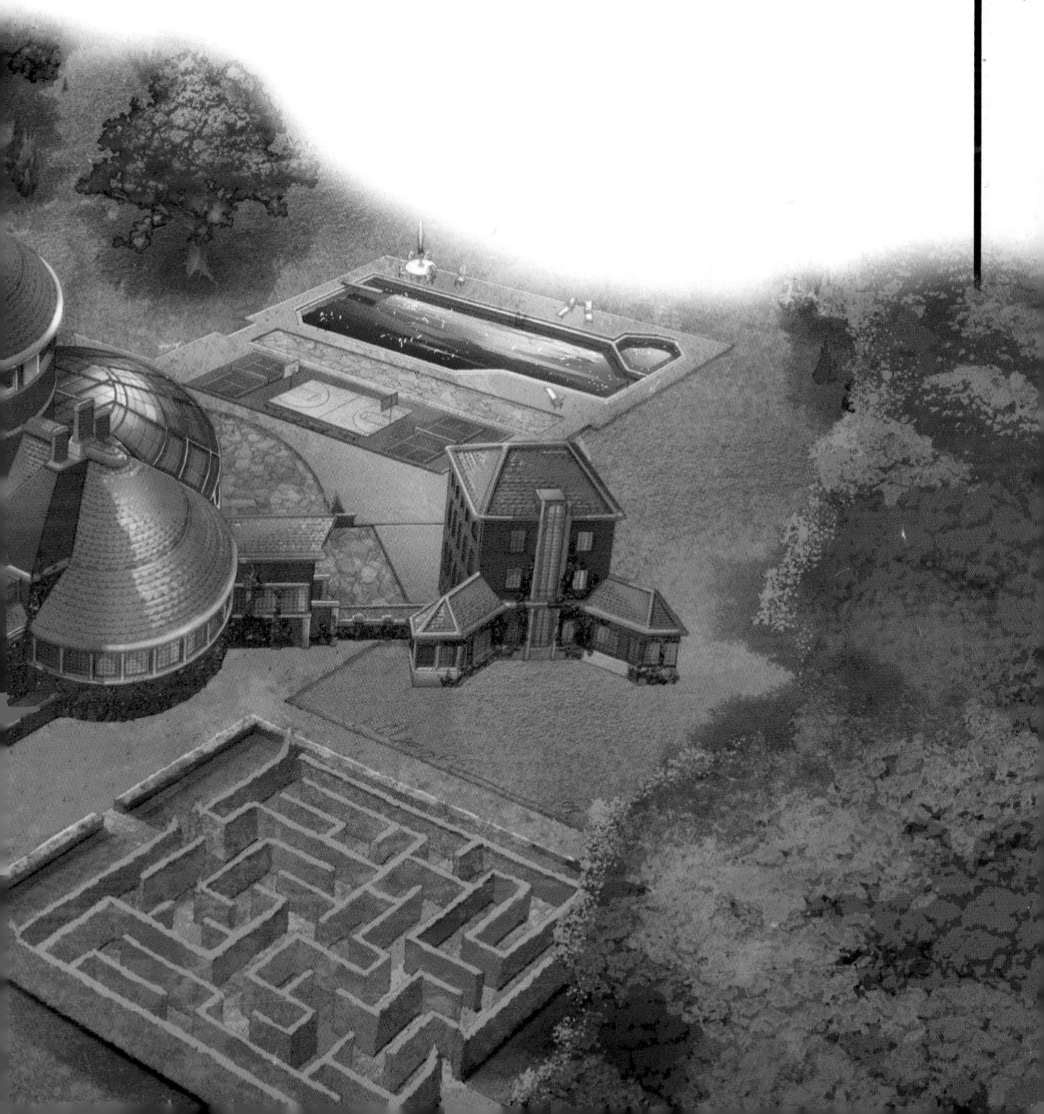

There is a secret, underground hangar hidden from view on the estate. The X-Men's jet, the Blackbird, is kept there. When the Blackbird is needed, it races along an underground runway, then takes off into the sky. A tractor beam guides the Blackbird safely back to the runway and also drives away unwanted visitors.

The Blackbird can also take off vertically through an opening in the underground hangar.

The Blackbird can even fly into space.

The mansion itself has dorms, classrooms, and a large kitchen. Professor X often teaches classes in the library. Special high-speed tubes carry students to the mansion's lower levels.

Monorail
An underground monorail zips the X-Men from the mansion to the secret Blackbird hangar in just 20 seconds!

The Danger Room

The most important part of
Professor X's training program takes
place in the Danger Room. This is
a special training area where
the X-Men work hard to improve their
athletic and fighting skills. It is the place
where mutants practice using
their powers during combat.

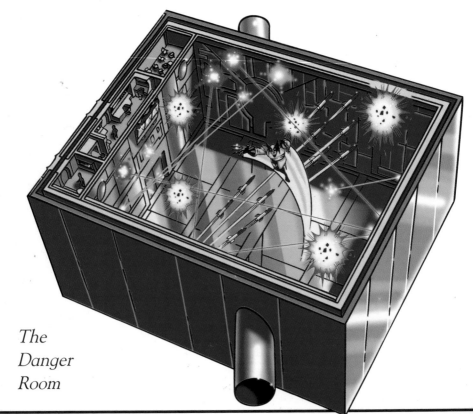

The
Danger
Room

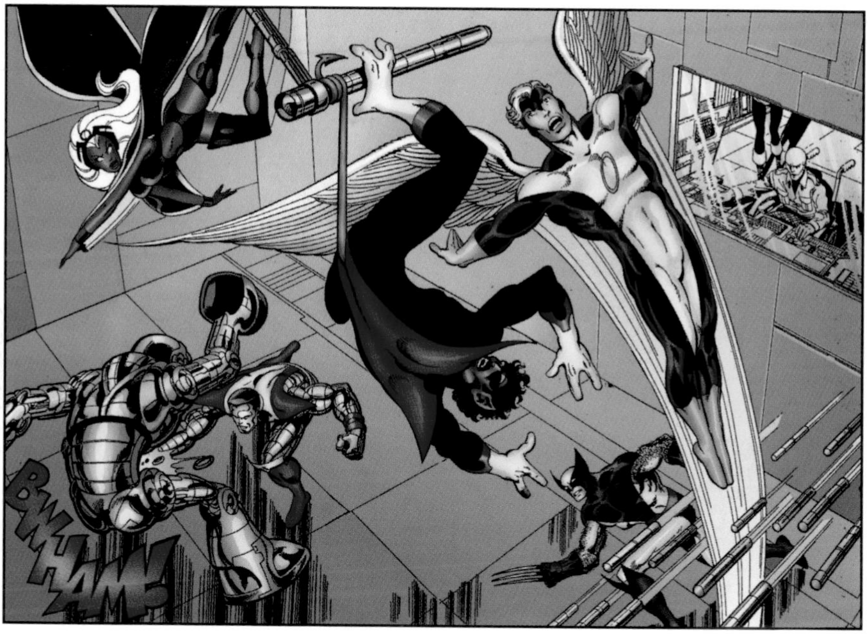
BWHAM!

Professor X controls special combat robots as they test the fighting skills of the X-Men in the Danger Room.

The Danger Room contains special equipment that challenges the X-Men. Professor X sits in the control room next to the Danger Room. From there, he can train his X-Men to deal with all kinds of danger. Missiles, lasers, and alien weapons attack the X-Men. They must react swiftly to these deadly assaults.

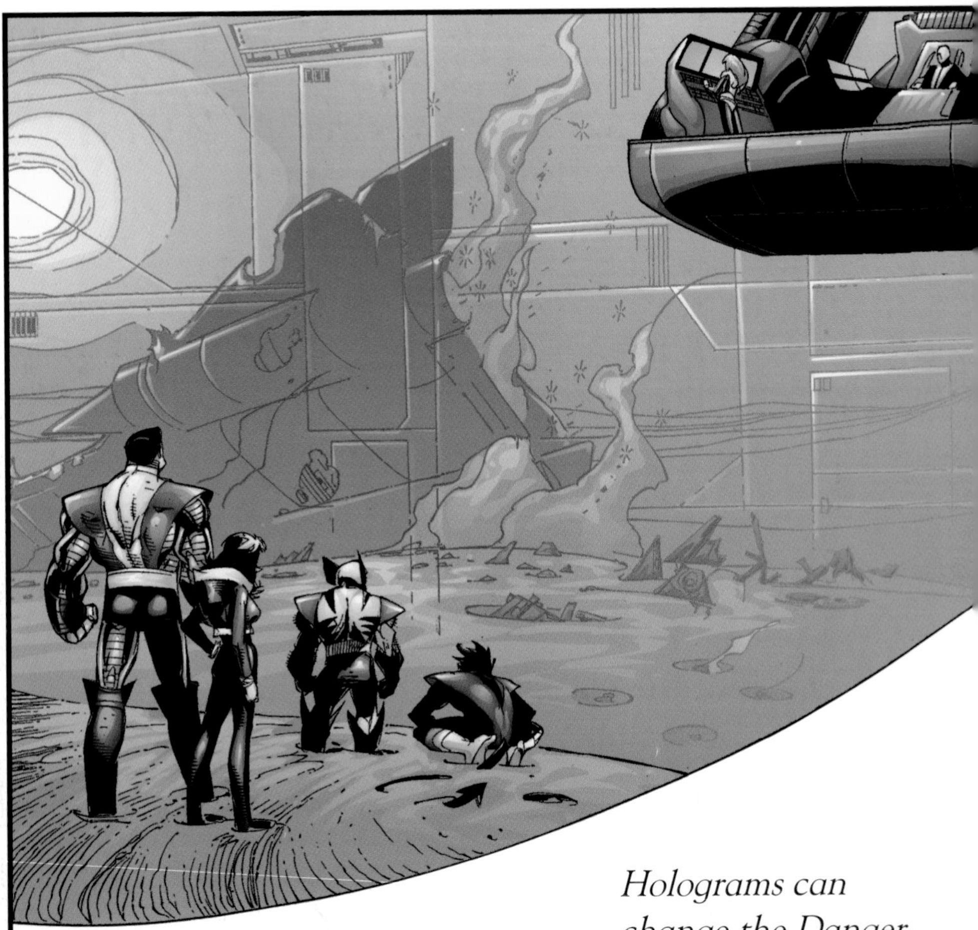

Holograms can change the Danger Room into anything.

Professor X sets traps to surprise his students. Steel nets, giant hammers, and a large vice with sharp metal teeth must be avoided. Metal tentacles and jets of flame sometimes lash out at the X-Men training in the Danger Room.

Mind machine
Cerebro is Professor X's super computer. When he is connected by a headset, it helps him to locate other mutants.

Right next to the Danger Room is the War Room. The War Room is filled with powerful computers, which collect information from around the world. Large screens in the War Room allow Professor X to keep an eye on his X-Men during actual combat situations.

The War Room

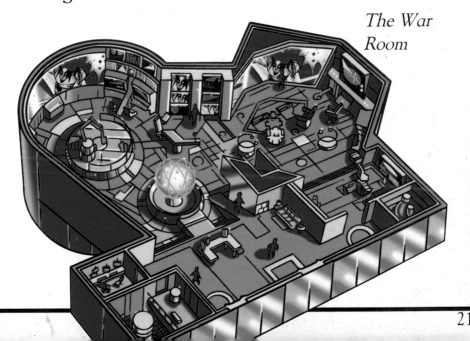

The first students

Scott Summers, also known as Cyclops, was the first student at Professor X's School for Gifted Youngsters. He quickly became Professor X's most trusted ally. Cyclops shares the professor's belief that humans and mutants should live together in peace. Cyclops most often leads the X-Men into battle.

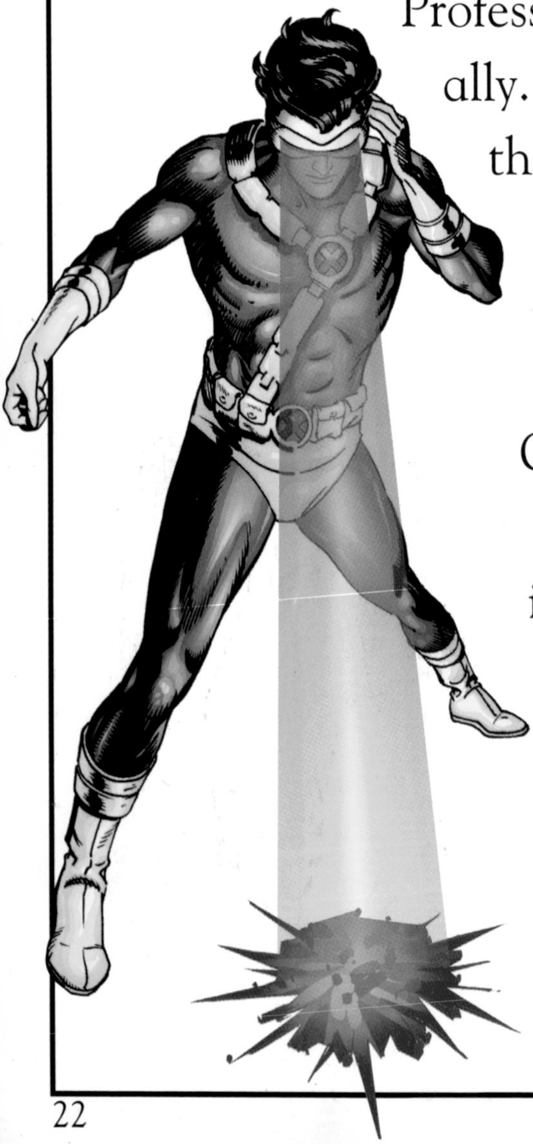

Cyclops absorbs his power from the sun. He uses it to fire ruby-red rays from his eyes.

Special visor
Cyclops's visor blocks his eye beams. He presses a button on either side of the visor to release his optic blasts.

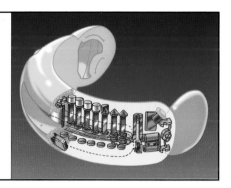

Cyclops's mutant power is the ability to shoot powerful beams from his eyes. These beams are so strong they can destroy an entire building. Cyclops must wear special glasses or a visor to stop the deadly beams.

The beams from Cyclops's eyes can destroy a tank!

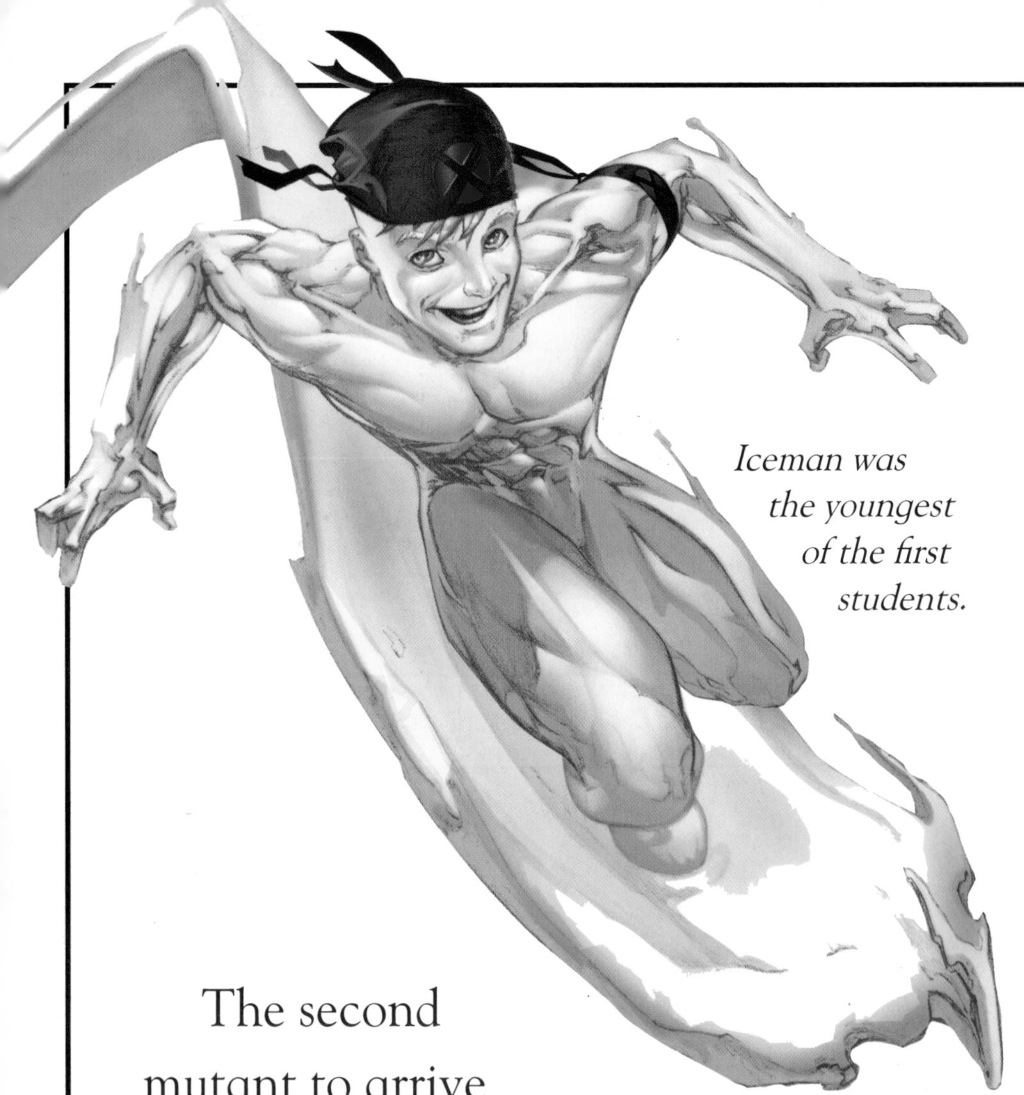

Iceman was the youngest of the first students.

The second mutant to arrive at the school and join the X-Men was Bobby Drake, known as Iceman. Iceman can freeze anything, including his own body. He can shape moisture from the air into an ice slide that lets him travel really fast.

The young Bobby Drake only used his freezing power as a last resort when his girlfriend was attacked.

Iceman discovered his powers in his early teens but kept them secret. One night, he used his icy skills to protect his girlfriend from an attacker. A frightened crowd then began attacking Bobby. He was rescued by Professor X and Cyclops, who invited him to become a student at the school.

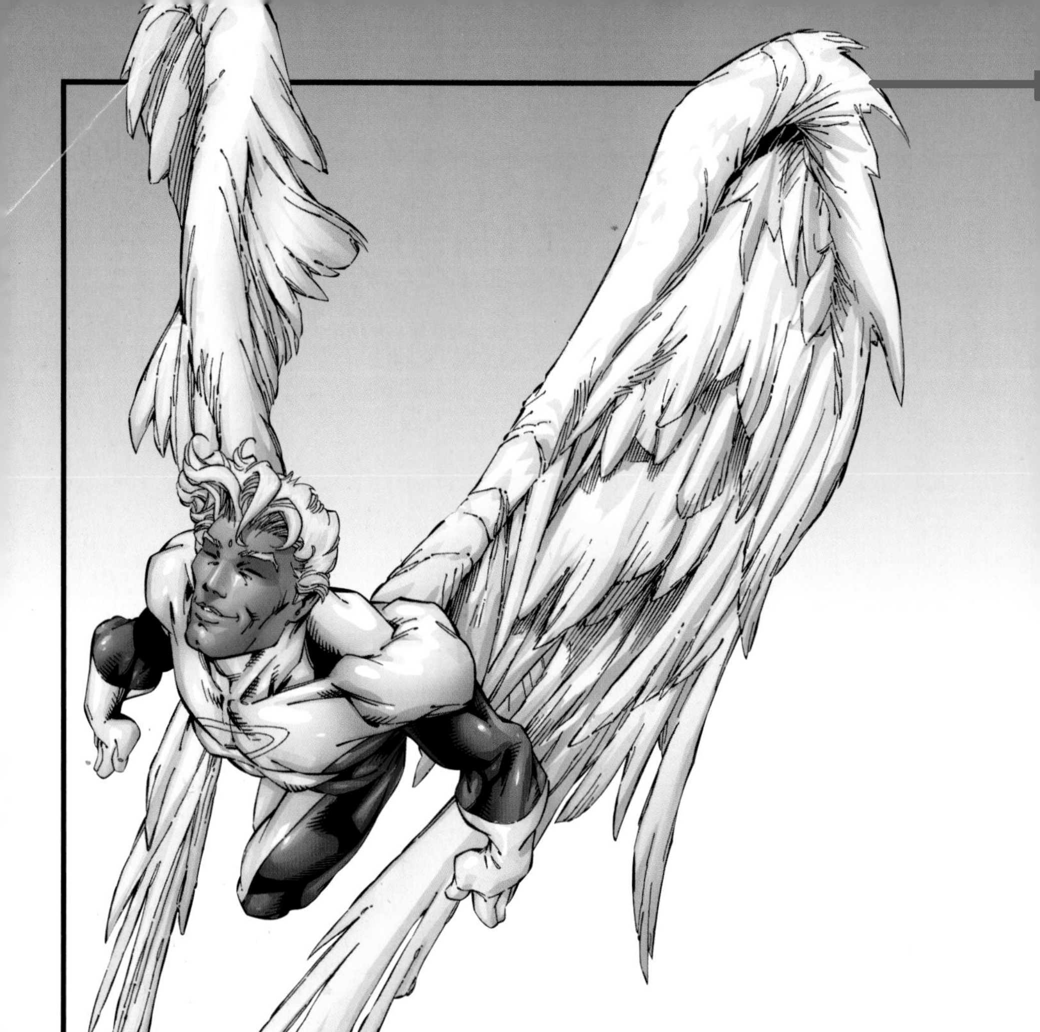

When Warren Worthington III was a teenager, something strange happened. He grew a pair of wings from his back. Discovering he was a mutant, Warren practiced in secret, learning how to fly using his wings.

Wings of an angel
Using his powerful wings,
Angel can soar to a height of
10,000 feet (3,000 meters).
His wings can fold up under
his clothes.

He went to New York City and became
a costumed crime fighter. Warren called
himself the Avenging Angel.

During this time, Professor X learned
of Warren's ability. He asked Warren
to come to
the school and
join the X-Men.
Warren agreed and
became known as
Angel and later as
Archangel.

*Like all the X-Men, Angel
is a fierce fighter!*

Hank McCoy's mutant powers allow him to run fast for long distances and swing from a tree like an acrobat. He is as strong as ten men and is also a brilliant scientist, with a mind almost as amazing as that of Professor X.

The professor invited Hank to join the original X-Men. He was called Beast because of his huge hands and feet.

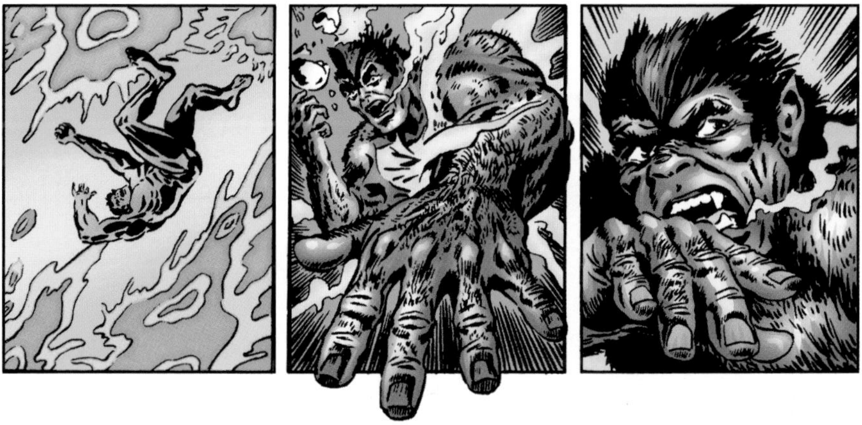

The formula changed Hank into a giant blue beast!

After he graduated from the school, Beast created a formula to help bring out hidden powers in mutants. When he drank the formula himself, he grew blue fur all over his body.

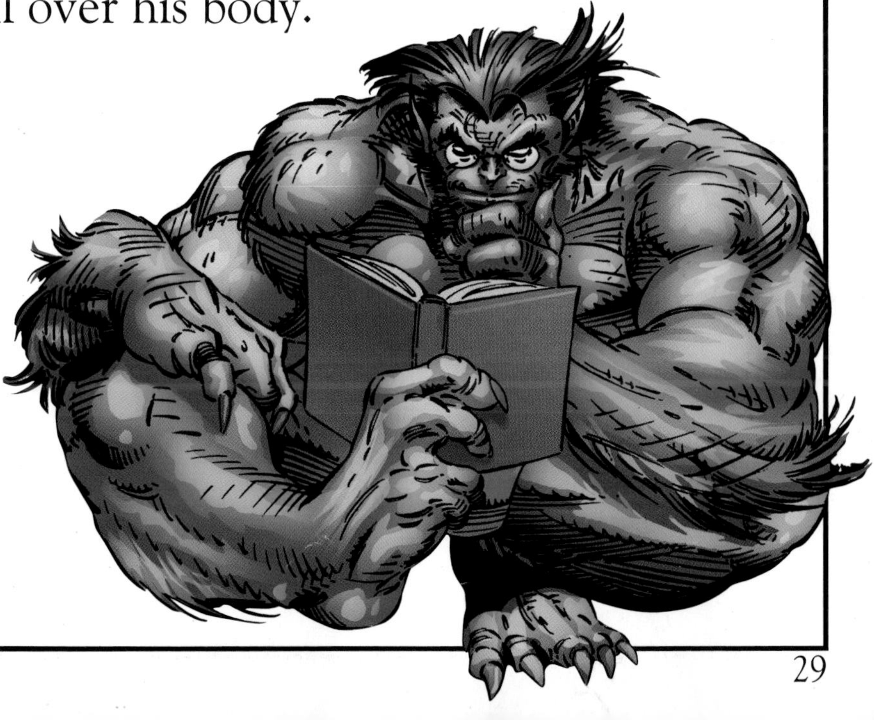

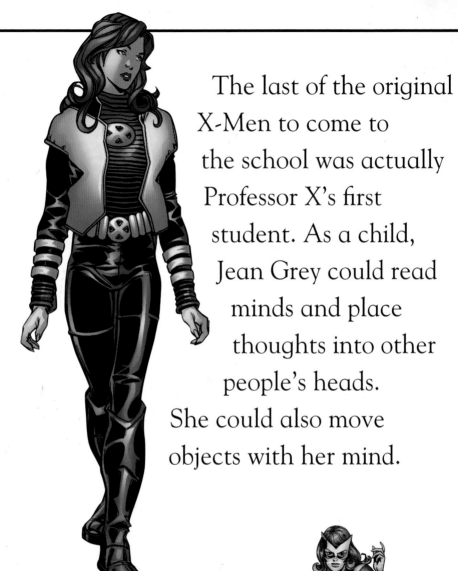

The last of the original X-Men to come to the school was actually Professor X's first student. As a child, Jean Grey could read minds and place thoughts into other people's heads. She could also move objects with her mind.

Name change
Jean Grey used the name Marvel Girl when she arrived at the school. Later, she was called Phoenix.

As Phoenix, Jean Grey has incredible power.

When she was eleven, Jean was injured by her own mental abilities. Her parents sent her to Professor X for help. He healed her and helped train her to use her powers. Later, Jean became a key member of the X-Men and a teacher at the school.

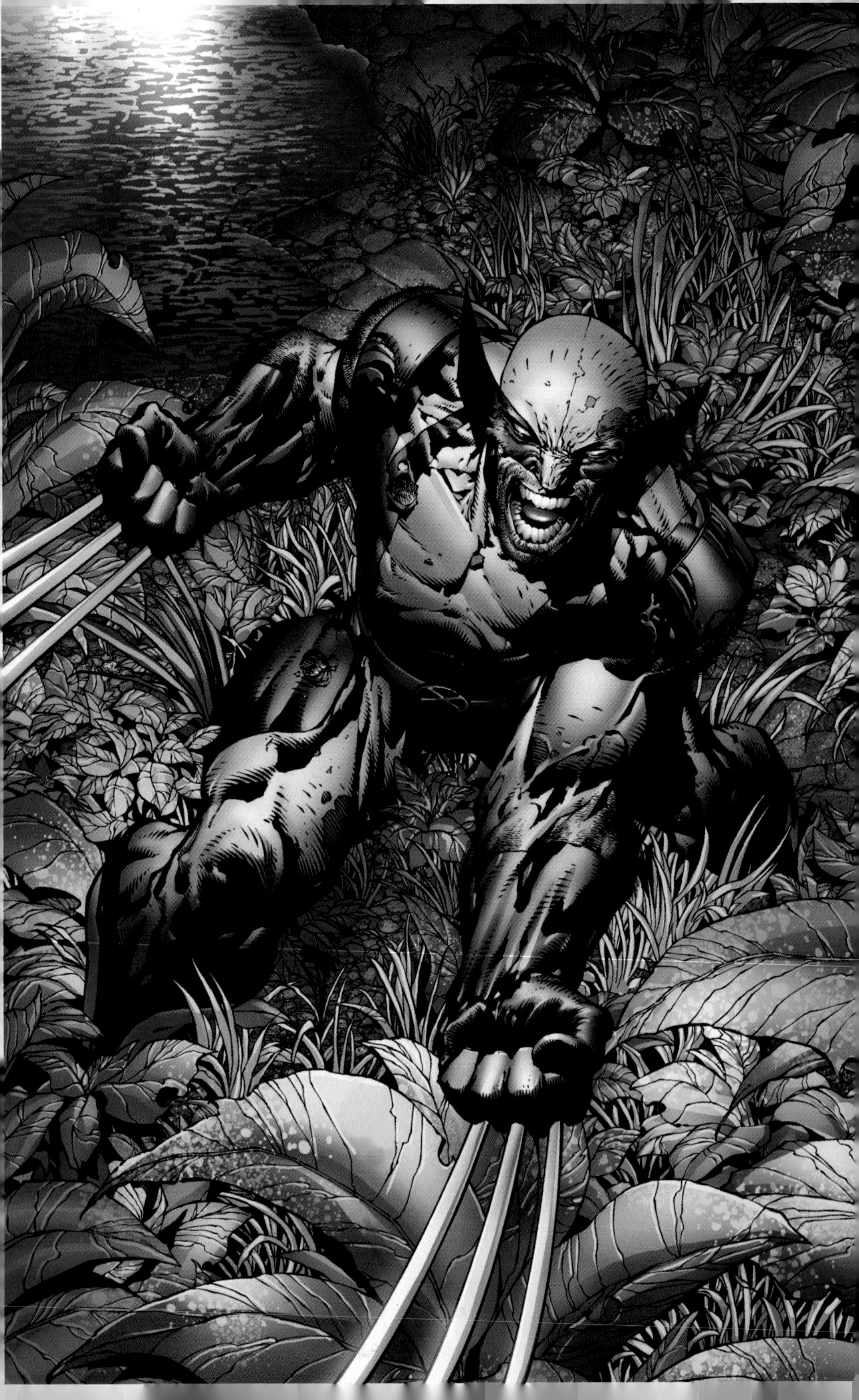

Famous graduates

Over the years, many mutants have come to study at the School for Gifted Youngsters. A number of them went on to become important members of the X-Men team.

Probably the most famous of all the X-Men is Wolverine. His real name is Logan, and he was born in Canada. As part of a secret government experiment, Wolverine was given a metal skeleton and long, sharp metal claws. Wolverine's mutant power is the ability to heal very quickly from any injury. His healing power, metal skeleton, and razor-sharp claws come in handy when he fights.

Wolverine got his name because he is a fierce fighter and can track down his enemies by smell like a wolf.

Another important member of the X-Men team is Ororo Munroe, also known as Storm. She has the power to control the weather. This mutant can create rain, snow, hail, wind, fog, or lightning. Storm's powers are connected to the way she feels. When she gets angry, dark clouds gather. If she is very upset, strong winds blow and thunder booms in the sky. At the School for Gifted Youngsters, Professor X taught her how to control her incredible ability. She teaches younger mutants at the school.

Storm was born in Africa.

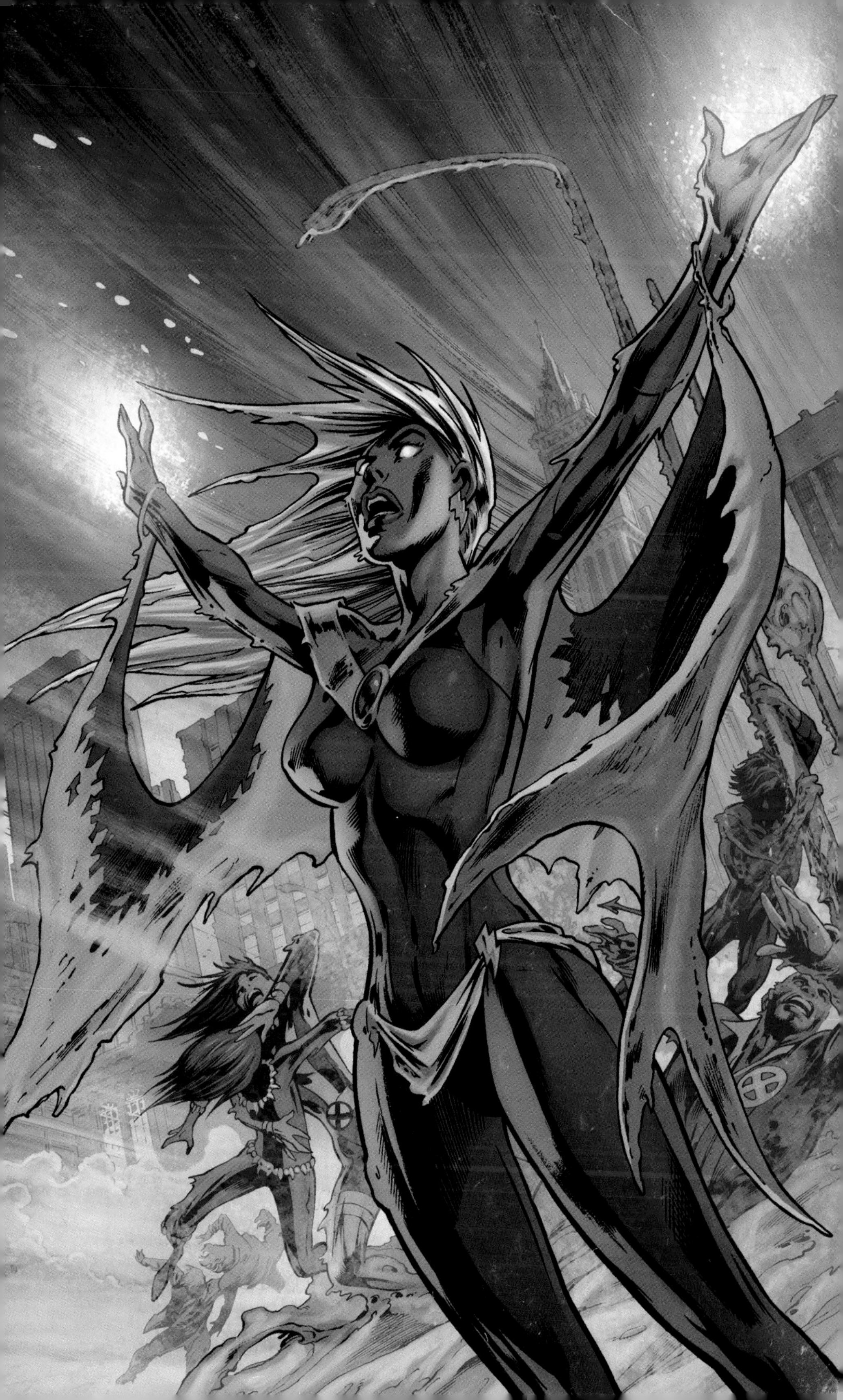

Rogue's mutant power is both a gift and a curse. She can absorb a person's memories and life energy just by touching them. But that touch can leave the person in a coma.

Rogue came to the school to get help from Professor X to control her absorbing power. She still cannot fully control it. So Rogue must cover her entire body at all times. She always wears gloves to be sure she doesn't accidentally touch and harm anyone.

Rogue can also absorb the powers of other mutants and Super Heroes, although the powers only last short time.

Rogue has incredible strength.

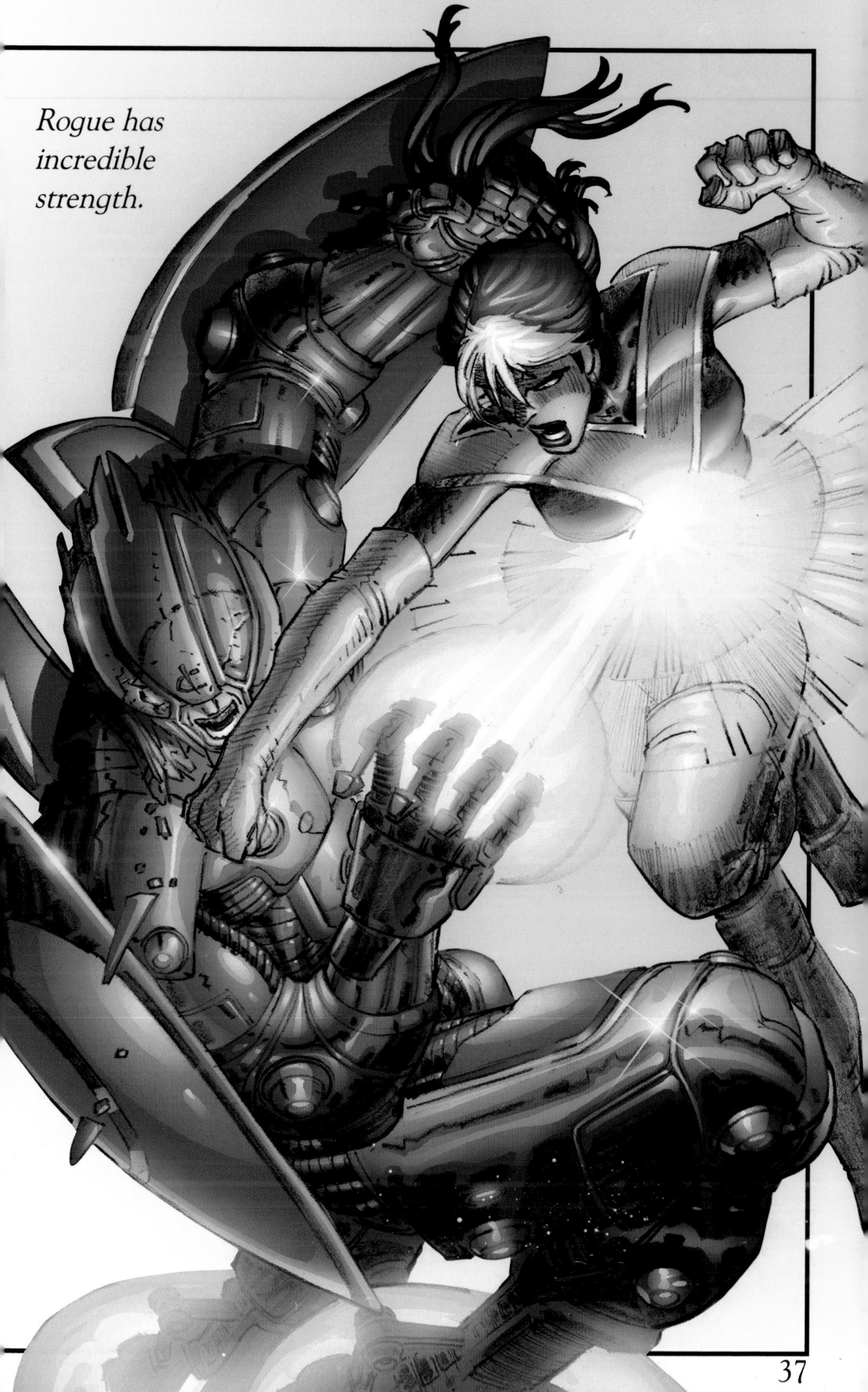

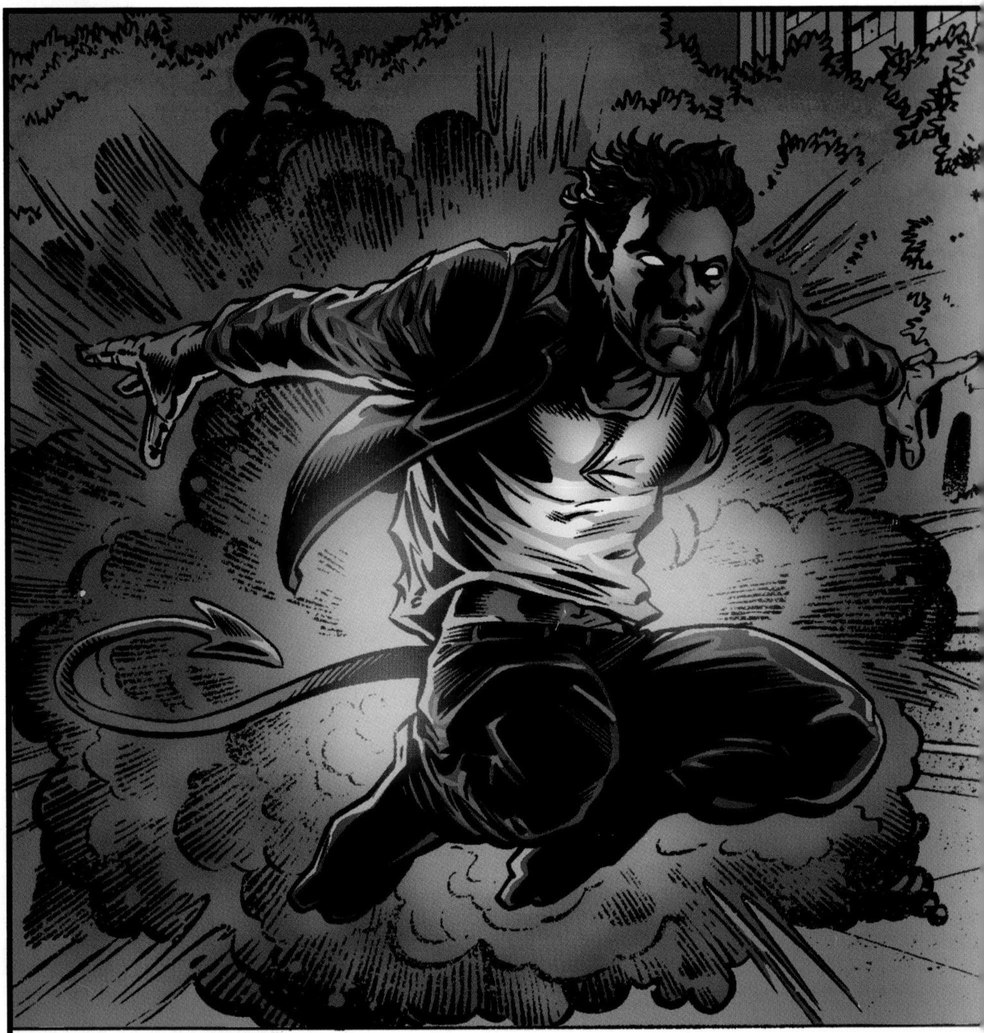

Nightcrawler has the power to teleport from one place to another in a split second. Now, he's there, and then—poof!—he vanishes in a puff of smoke, only to reappear in another spot!

Nightcrawler, whose real name is
Kurt Wagner, was born in Germany.
There, he was feared by the villagers
in his small town. They were frightened
by his teleporting power and by
the way he looked.

Professor X
invited him to come
to the school and
join the X-Men.
Like many
other mutants,
Nightcrawler
found a safe home
within the walls of
the X-Men mansion.

*Professor X saved Nightcrawler from the angry villagers
who were trying to kill him.*

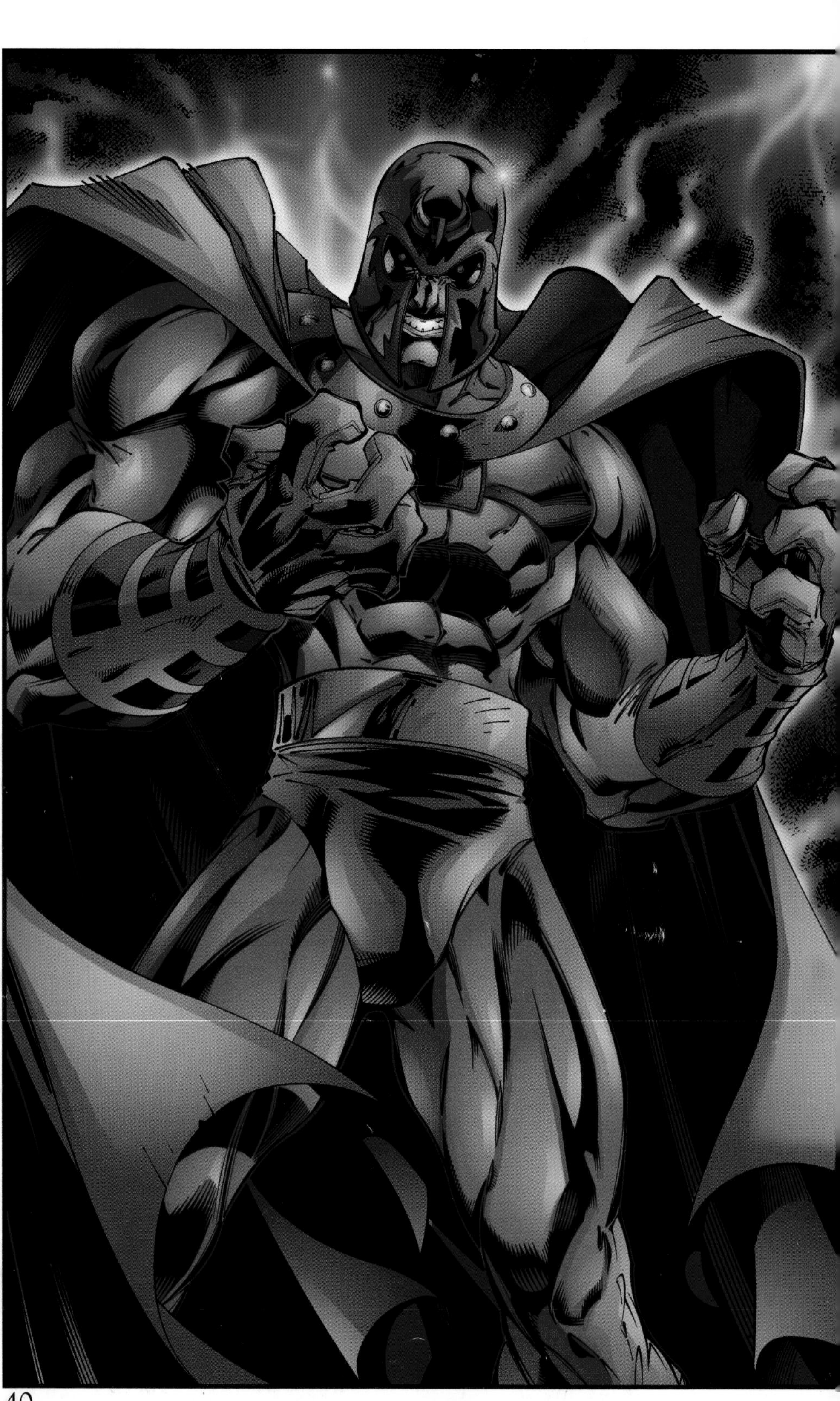

Magneto

Professor X started his School for Gifted Youngsters to give mutants a safe home and help train them to use their powers. But he also began the school to stop the mutant Magneto.

Magneto does not believe that humans and mutants should live together in peace. He believes that mutants should destroy humans and take over the Earth. Magneto is the greatest threat to Professor X's dream of mutants and humans getting along together.

Professor X and Magneto are deadly enemies.

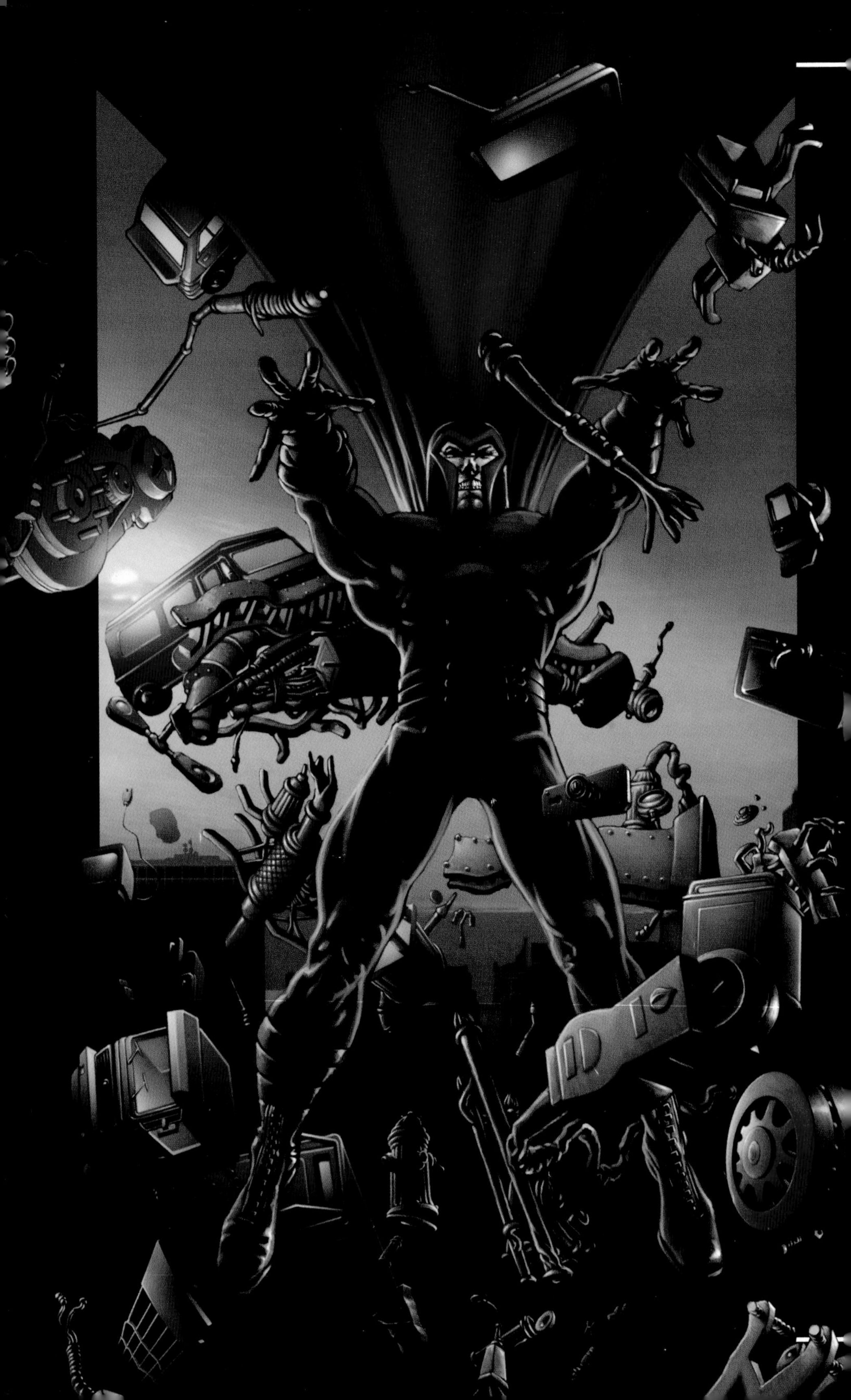

Magneto is known as the Master of Magnetism. His mutant power is the ability to control metal objects using his magnetic force.

Magneto and Professor X started out as friends. Soon, Magneto's belief that humans should be controlled by mutants made them enemies. Professor X hopes that one day his old friend will see things his way, but for now the battle between the X-Men and Magneto continues.

Mind protector
Magneto's helmet protects him from telepathic attacks. It prevents mutants like Professor X or Jean Grey from reading his mind or controlling his actions.

Generation X

Professor X's School for Gifted Youngsters has been a huge success. For many years, mutants from all over the world have come to the school. They have found a home and a place to develop their special talents.

In time, Professor X got too busy leading the X-Men to also run the school for younger mutants. He moved the school to Massachusetts and gave the running of the school to two experienced X-Men—Sean Cassidy, known as Banshee, and Emma Frost, known as the White Queen. Together, they teach the young mutants known as Generation X.

The mutants of Generation X come from all over the world and have many different powers.

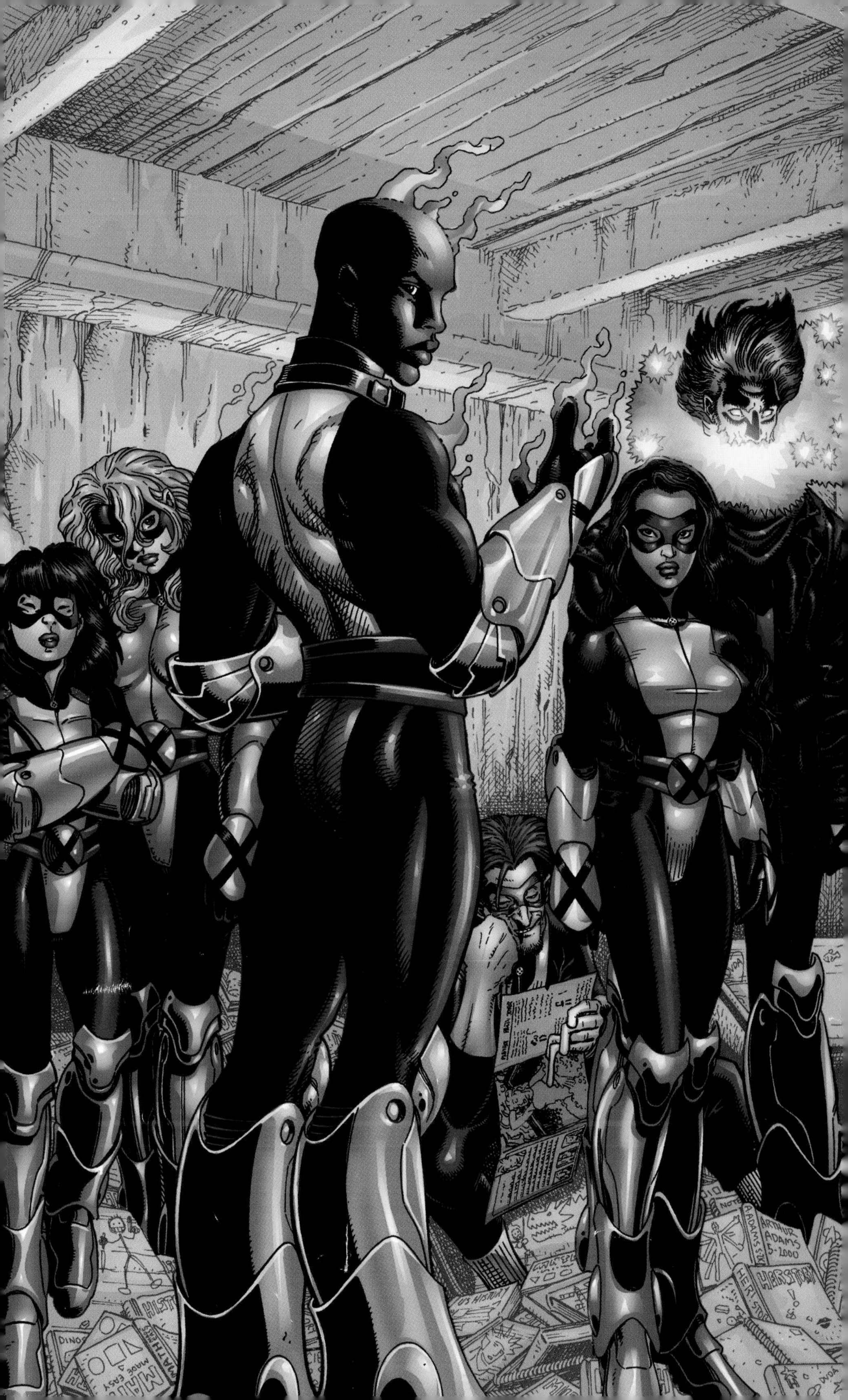

ARTHUR ADAMS 5-2000
HERSTORY
US HISTORY
MATH MADE EASY
DINOS

At the new school, the students of Generation X are taught to control their powers and use them for good.

Professor X's dedication to teaching didn't stop when the school moved. He turned his mansion into the Xavier Institute for Higher Learning. There, more experienced mutants could study and improve their skills.

Through both X-Men schools, Professor X hopes his dream of humans and mutants living together in peace will someday come true.

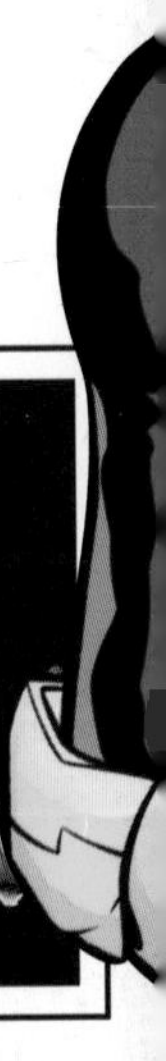

X enemy
The White Queen used to be the X-Men's enemy. In time, she accepted the idea of humans and mutants working together.

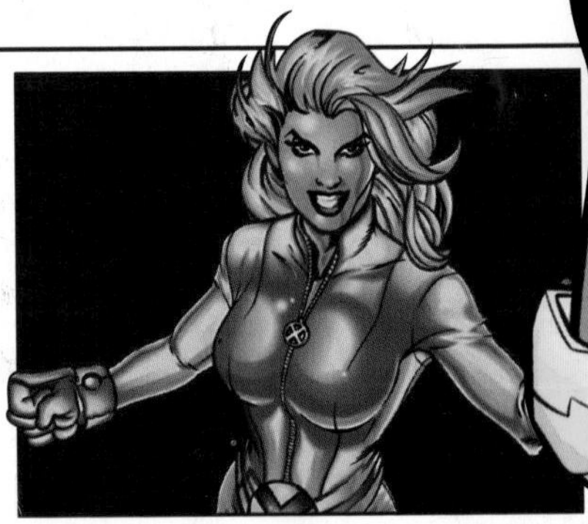

Some of the teenage mutants who make up Generation X. They use their mutant powers to help fight the enemies of the X-Men.

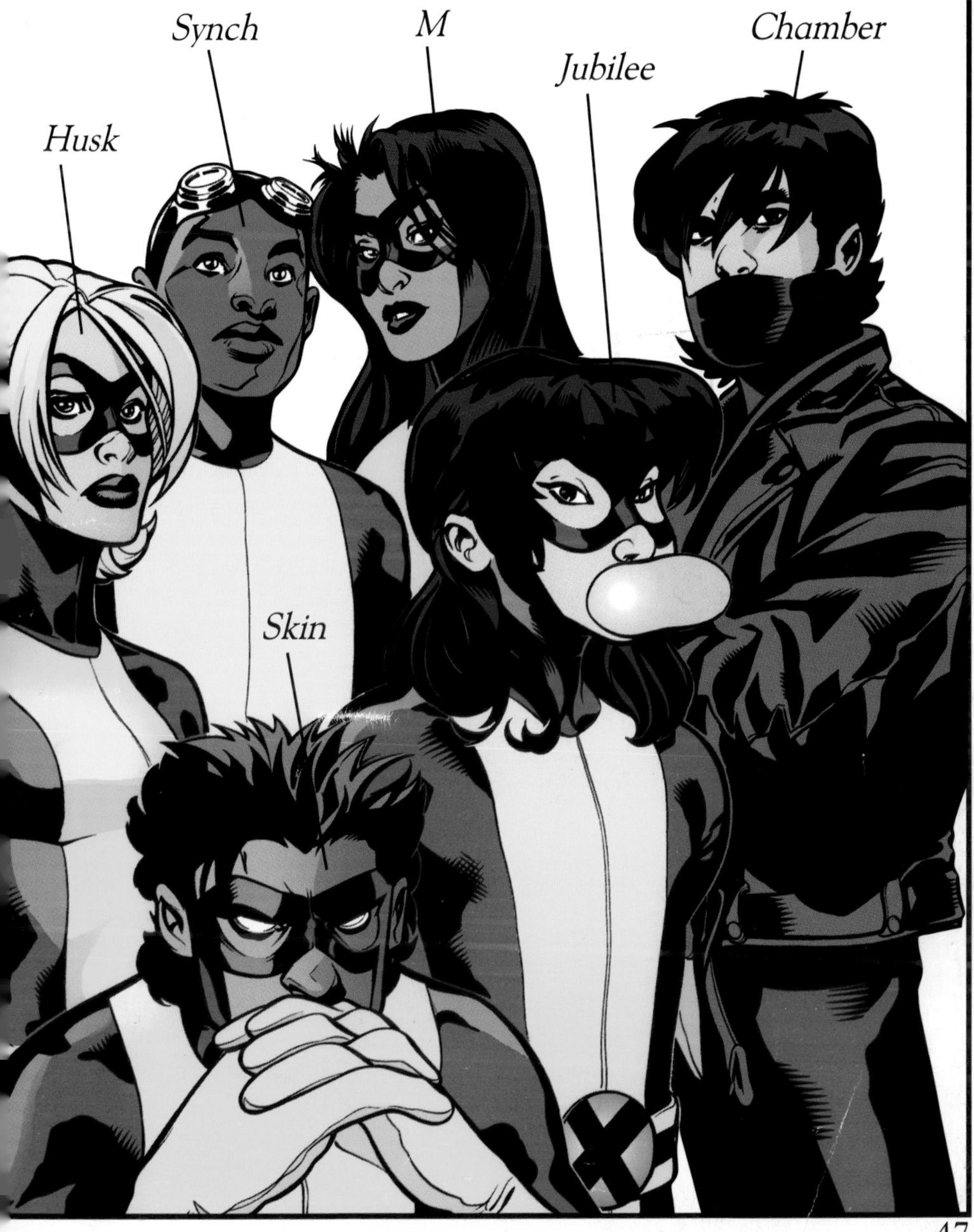
Synch
M
Chamber
Jubilee
Husk
Skin

Glossary

acrobat
A circus performer who swings from ropes and trapezes.

alien
A creature who is not human and comes from outer space.

ally
A friend or helper.

assaults
Violent attacks on a person or persons.

challenges
Tests someones skills.

coma
A state of unconsciousness, a bit like sleeping. It is caused by illness or injury.

combat
A fight.

curse
A cause of bad luck.

dedication
Commitment or determination to do something.

dorms
Large rooms where students sleep.

emerge
Appear.

estate
A large piece of land, usually with a house and many buildings on it.

evolved
Changed very slowly. Humans evolved from apes.

graduates
Students who have finished studying at a school or college.

hangar
A building where aircraft are kept.

holograms
Three-dimensional images made from light that look real.

magnetic force
A power that makes some metals attract each other.

memories
Thoughts of the past.

mental
To do with the mind.

moisture
Water in the form of tiny droplets.

optic
To do with the eyes.

original
The first.

prejudice
Hating people because they are different from you.

security
Protection against danger.

teleport
Move instantly from one place to another.

tentacles
Long arms that bend easily.

vice
A metal tool like a clamp used to hold on to something tightly.

visor
A screen in front of the eyes.

Index